Strategic STAGING TIPS

For Home Sellers

Top Home Stager Reveals:

The Secrets On How To Have Your Home Ready To Sell

*For **TOP Dollar**...Even In A **DOWN Market**!*

Justin LaFavor with Jill Gargus

Please direct any inquiries to:
Justin LaFavor - justin@edmonton-real-estate-online.com
Jill Gargus - homestaging@telus.net

DISCLOSURE: Both of the authors are Licensed Real Estate Associates in the Province of Alberta. This material is not intended to interfere with an existing agency agreement/relationship the reader may have with another brokerage.

DEDICATIONS & THANKS

From Jill Gargus...

"*I would like to first and most importantly, thank Jesus Christ for blessing me with opportunities and these talents. He gives me the strength to carry them out.*

Also thank you to my mom, Randee, who is my tireless sounding board and supporter.

As well, thanks to my entire team of subcontractors. Without their help, team attitude and faithfulness I would not be able to do all of this. They are everything to me, Thank you!

And thank you to Justin La Favor for thinking of me to help write this book, a "God timed meeting" for sure...What a pleasure it has been to work with you, so much fun!"

From Justin La Favor...

"*First things first - I give all the credit to God for how He's blessed my life so abundantly. It's only by His grace that I'm able to do what I do (Deut. 8:18!!).*

Next, to my beautiful and loving wife Kate - Your patience with my busy work schedule, your dedication to our family, and your encouragement for me to pursue becoming an author, I truly could not have done it (and cannot do it!) without you. I love you!

Lastly, thanks to Jill for agreeing to come onboard for such a ground-breaking project in both of our industries. I couldn't believe how quickly God can answer a prayer when, not five minutes after I had finished thinking about who my top pick would be to approach for this book, I run into you coming off the elevator at my office! I'm truly blessed to be able to partner with the proprietor of Western Canada's Leading Home Staging Company, and to those who are reading this section, you are truly getting info from the best lady in the business!"

CONTENTS

CHAPTER 1

Does Curb Appeal Really Matter?

"As a home stager, when you are looking at a house from the curb, what are some of your strategies on enhancing curb appeal?"

Jill says:

A buyer decides within seconds whether they want to view the interior of a property, based on what the outside appearance "says". So I tell my clients to do all regular yard care as their foundational point. This includes grass/snow care, mulching, weeding, garbage removal and all obvious repairs, including a fresh coat of paint if required and weather permitting. We then take it to the next step and go to **wow factor**. This can be obtained by adding color, although no more than three overall. A tip I give is to scope out the new home subdivisions and see what colors they are using and then do the same. This will help your home to stand out more. I call it "Drive By Staging"!!

When choosing three exterior colors, start at the top and use the shingle color to work from as it carries the most visual weight. We can then build two more colors into the picture, not including greenery. For example: shutters and rock work may be one color of reddish brown and the siding a light beige and the roofing a chocolate brown. This will work well together and tie the entire look together.

Adding small pops of the reddish brown and chocolate color can be reached by flower pots, small furniture/cushions if space allows, a properly positioned entry rug that fits the space, and greens. Greenery always wins and brings vibrancy to the overall picture.

And a freshly painted front door that is a bolder color always wins hearts. Keep the area free of all garbage and extra items that are not required for staging. A new door knocker, kick plate and exterior lighting, new shiny numbers and mailbox also say "*Welcome to Your New Home!*"

JUSTIN'S COMMENTS:

I can't count how many times I've driven up to a home with a buyer in my vehicle and, based solely on the exterior appearance, they've quickly said *"Umm...NO THANKS"* and we turned around and never set foot on the property.

Investing in these details on the exterior of your home can be the difference between a real estate agent calling to book a second showing, or calling to apologize that their client opted to not even see the interior of the home based on the shabby exterior.

The old saying *"It's what's inside that counts"* is totally useless when selling your home. The **TOTAL PACKAGE** is what counts. Sellers who take advice like Jill has just outlined will ensure that their home's total package stands out from the competition.

BEFORE

ACTUAL WORK BY JILL'S TEAM:

"Curb appeal with minimum cost and maximum effect.

We changed the mint green trim to black to tie into the red and black in the bricks.

We also weeded, mulched in black and cleaned the exterior.

The client had grass care done and added flowers to the front step.

We also painted the front door black to tie it all in."

AFTER

BEFORE

AFTER

CHAPTER 2

Making A Solid First Impression

"Jill, in your opinion, how important is it to make a solid first-impression when a buyer walks into the main entrance?? How do you advise clients as to what they can do to achieve this positive first impression?"

Jill says:

A solid first impression is critical as a buyer's initial perceptions of the home are formed in the first few seconds. A number of factors contribute to this, such as what they see, smell and feel.

The first step into a property gives an immediate overall picture of more than one room, so every room needs to present well, not just an entry. The main sight lines often include the entry, living and dining room, part of the kitchen and perhaps a staircase.

Beginning by staging an entry way with fresh paint, a new rug, art or a mirror and table is a great place to start. Additionally, consider the smells a buyer will notice, as a closet full of smelly sporting gear or footwear is no way to make a great first 'smell' impression. I advise clients to remove all odor producing items, including pet related ones and when at their home I specifically speak to anything I notice, including repair items and cleanliness.

As the old adage goes: "*You never get a second chance to make a first impression.*"

JUSTIN'S COMMENTS:

They say that when a person meets another person for the first time, it takes 3-5 seconds to form a lasting first-impression of that person, and that it's very hard to alter that initial impression even if subsequent interactions are positive.

Now consider this: When you meet someone, usually it's for FREE and you're not considering spending hundreds of thousands of dollars on that person!

When preparing your house for sale, you need to keep in mind that making a good first impression on the buyer is IMPERATIVE if they're to come back and make an offer. After all, if you're not giving your house to them for free, you need to give them as many reasons as possible why your home is the nicest one for them!

ACTUAL WORK BY JILL'S TEAM:

"This dining room was painted red and yellow like McDonald's®, yet had beautiful slate tile and a river valley view.

I pulled a color from the floor and repainted, added furniture and created a look that was better suited to the price point."

BEFORE

AFTER

CHAPTER 3

How To Get The Best ROI On Reno's

*"If I'm debating whether or not to renovate
a room or part of a room, what criteria
should I use to ensure I get the best
Return On Investment?"*

Jill says:

Your ROI is determined by the market and returns that have been previously obtained by sellers across the country. Research done by national surveys on this subject, is outlined on my website at www.stageandsell.ca and can also be viewed on www.homegain.com

Typically upgrades that fall under a "maintenance category" are items that bring the lowest return on investment. It is expected that over the years, owners will pay to make those upgrades and maintain the condition of the property. This includes things like upgrades of electrical, plumbing, kitchens and baths and other necessary repairs. Regular upkeep over the life of your property ownership should reflect 1-3% every year of it's market value in order to be priced at market value when you go to sell. This is important to note, and is an often unconsidered aspect of pricing when it's time to sell.

However, when staging, things like de-cluttering, lighting and staging bring a higher rate of return as a buyer then connects emotionally with your property, envisioning themselves living there. Staging as a marketing tool mainly, brings an 80% ROI as it creates a "lifestyle" in the mind of the buyer and all things being equal with your competition, yours will stand out as it hits their heart and motivates them to write an offer.

JUSTIN'S COMMENTS:

While "maintenance items" may bring the lowest ROI compared to Home Staging, it's unfortunate that many home owners end up neglecting these items and still expect to sell their home for top dollar, when competing properties are boasting that they do have standard upgrades completed in their home (electrical, windows, roof, furnace, hot water tank, etc.)

It never hurts to get professional advice from your team when deciding to renovate a room or part of a room. It might make sense to allocate a large part of your budget for upgrades to your property, and spend the remainder on having your home staged. Or it might be wise to go the other way around and spend more money on staging if your home already has upgrades that make it competitive in your marketplace.

Each home is a unique situation, and every home seller will have unique circumstances. Only by discussing these with your team of trusted advisors will you be able to come up with a solution.

One thing is for sure though, I've never yet had a client who staged their home not reap multiple benefits from what they invested by hiring a professional Home Stager.

CHAPTER 4

What To Do On A Tight Budget

"If I have a limited budget, should I take a micro-approach and focus on a specific room/room(s) or should I take a macro-approach and focus on spreading my budget throughout the home in order to make the best first impression on buyers?"

Jill says:

The overall first impression from curb appeal to every room needs to be considered as it is the whole house that sells, not just one room. Take your budget and spread it over the preparation and included repairs. Then you are ready to add in the wow factor through staging.

A lot of what can be accomplished in the "homework" prep phase can be done by a willing homeowner with their sweat equity. If they don't do that, a buyer will not clean up a seller's mess unless they get the house for a rock bottom price. So you, as a seller, can decide to pull up your boot straps and get to it. Sweat equity is hard, but it pays off in the end. If you don't prepare your property, today's buyers will just move to one that has been made ready and offers them more perks than yours does.

After prep is done, use your budget to bring in a fresh paint color and accessories. You can still use your own furniture if it is in good shape. This is where a home Stager can walk in and finish the project for you, if you are too intimidated. Expect to spend up to $5,000 to prepare your house, depending on how much you haven't been keeping it up over the years. Remember, staging is usually less than your FIRST price reduction and the goal is to not have price reductions or go stale on the market. This $5,000 can be for repairs, updates to lighting, staging, yard clean up, carpet cleaning, rentals of accessories from a Home Stager, cleaning and even for storage.

JUSTIN'S COMMENTS:

What if I told you that you could make $100/hour cleaning your oven? Wiping your microwave down? Scrubbing your bath tub? Would you believe me?

Well, in many circumstances, it's totally possible to realize this type of return when you invest some elbow grease into maximizing your sweat equity. Although nobody loves doing dirty work, if your family spent just 10 hours over a weekend to make your home sparkle, I'd be confident the overall impression your home will have on a buyer will exceed an extra $1000 at selling time.

Don't have time? Then spend a couple hundred dollars and hire a professional to come and do the work. While this might seem like an extravagance, think about it as spending $100 for a cleaner, and seeing $1000 extra at closing. That's a 10-to-1 return...Better than mutual funds!

CHAPTER 5

The BIGGEST Mistake You DON'T Want To Make!

"What is the biggest mistake that sellers make when trying to stage their home on their own without the help of a professional home stager?"

Jill says:

The biggest mistake home sellers make is missing the last step of actual staging. Staging is the final drum roll, the "Grande Finale"!

Creating wow factor takes talent that is born out of natural staging ability and marketing education. Most sellers can handle step two which includes the homework of de-cluttering, cleaning, repairs, minor upgrades and paint, but when it comes to how to put a visually pleasing product together in the shape of a room, they miss they mark. Theory and copy can only go so far.

Many sellers think when it's clean, repaired, and decorated that it looks pretty good. It may, but after all the effort to prepare for step three (the Staging) and then to fall short on that point is like a wedding cake with no icing. It's just a cake. No "wow".

Hiring a professional Home Staging company is well worth the price given the financial gain in the end. It's a costly mistake to leave that most crucial piece out of the puzzle.

Professional Staging helps take even the most mundane rooms (Such as this shot of a basic Bed + Side Table) and give it the "WOW" Factor that captures the Buyer's attention and helps them envision what it's like to be *living* in that space.

Advertising copywriters call this concept "Future Pacing" and professional Home Staging is quite literally "Future-Pacing In-Person"!

JUSTIN'S COMMENTS:

I've had clients sell their home and try to stage it themselves. And while I've got to admit, some of them have impeccable taste and actually did a decent job arranging things on their own without hiring a professional Home Stager, these are the rare exception.

Even with the results that my clients achieved by naturally having "good sense" of design and décor, as their real estate agent I still would have preferred they invest in the services of a Home Stager as I believe it would've made a noticeable difference on their bottom line, either by selling in less time or selling for more than they ended up getting.

It's a different story if you simply can't afford to invest in a Home Stager. But if you can, even if it's a stretch, and are just choosing not to, I would encourage you to rethink your position. Your equity is at stake and sometimes, you need to spend a dollar to make two or three in return.

CHAPTER 6

A Mental Checklist For Preparing Your Home To SELL

"When you walk into any home, what are the 'mental checklist' of items that you go through as far as deciding what to change?"

Jill says:

The overall first impression is vital to me, as I am representing your "Buyer's Eyes". So I quickly assess what outdoor details are in need of attention as well as the initial first impression of the interior.

Smells, paint colors, cleanliness and clutter are the first to be noted.

Then my eyes move to deeper detail as I follow a strict outline for each room's assessment during the consultation. Right down to scratches on the backs of bedroom doors. Every detail of a house should be as spanky clean and pretty as a brand new car coming off the lot....nothing missed.

A Few More Direct Questions:

"Smells - What are offensive smells that you notice most often? What are their sources? What is your solution?"

"Paint Colors - What are the BEST colors for staging? Why? What would you say if somebody says they still live there and didn't like that color? Are bold colors a bad thing to have?"

"Cleanliness - What are typical spots that home sellers miss when it comes to keeping a house clean?"

"Clutter - What are your simple and easy solutions for clutter?"

SMELLS

The most offensive smells are body odor, and full kitty litter, as well as cooking smells like fish or curry and of course cigarette smoke.

To remove these smells first the offending issue has to be dealt with, then an air cleaner or ionizer can be brought in to start the purification process. Cleaning carpets, washing and painting walls and ceilings and of course fresh air can all help remove odors.

Sellers need to understand that their home needs to be a breath of fresh air to every potential new owner. They need to put themselves in the buyer's shoes by remembering what they were looking for when they were buying their home.

COLOR

There is no best staging color, because color choices are dependent on lighting, fixed elements and natural exposure. So when I choose a color it is usually never the same one from property to property, as each home has various elements that will affect my choice.

When doing a Home Staging project, the seller doesn't chose a color, I do. This is because we are marketing and they are moving. So the color is not for them to live with, it is to create appeal for a buyer. In fact it's a good measure for a real estate agent to know if the seller is serious about selling because if they are not that serious they usually will not let me choose a color.

The wildest colors we have painted over are hot pink, lime green and purple triangles in a teenagers room, very fun for her, but not great for selling!

CLEANLINESS

Cleanliness is essential in Staging, in fact everything should be 'white glove' clean. Areas that are usually overlooked are toilets, baseboards, interiors of cabinets and laundry areas. It needs to be so clean, it looks brand new.

CLUTTER

Clutter is always relative. What one person views as cluttered may not be to another. However in Home Staging there are principals we follow:

1. Anything that is personal or has names on it, like mail, diplomas, awards
2. All collections (eg. Coca Cola® items, dolls, Disney® & everything in between)
3. All religious material, statues, books
4. All seasonal and holiday items.
5. All cultural/political items.
6. All themed decorating such as wall paper boarders, specific themes, gender specific colored rooms
7. Extra sets of anything...keep only what you need out while you are selling
8. Evidence of cats, dogs, etc.

JUSTIN'S COMMENTS:

Here's a quick checklist review for your benefit, based on Jill's advice:

TO CHECK IN EACH ROOM:
- -> Corners: Any scratches/dents/chipped paint?
- -> Wall Surfaces: Any holes/dents/discoloration/stains?
- -> Trim: Any gaps? Nail holes filled? Cracks filled?
- -> Door: Is the doorknob loose? Scratches?
- -> Flooring: Any stains? Dents? Ripped/damaged patches?
- -> Smells: Any predominant odors?
- -> Colors: Does this room look like a magazine? Or are there crazy colors present? (lime green, hot pink, etc...)
- -> Clutter: Have I removed the items Jill mentions? (See list of previous page)
- -> Cleanliness: Have I cleaned around the toilet, tub, inside of cabinets, mirrors, laundry areas, hard-to-reach spots?

CHAPTER 7

Furniture & Related Issues

"Jill - I've got really big comfy furniture, but my real estate agent told me that it overwhelms the room. I like it, but what sort of dimensions or 'flow' should one aim for with staging a living room?"

Jill says:

Furniture scale is important to every room, as it has to look pleasing and have visual balance. Each property is assessed at the consultation for its needs and editing some pieces may be required to achieve the goal.

Furniture scale is always different in every job, so there is no hard and fast rule except to say the scale needs to fit. A couch should not be the elephant in the room, but just part of the entire picture. It should also allow for traffic patterns to naturally flow and not impede buyers from getting across the room.

We always take the whole picture into consideration when Staging and so should you. Extra or bulky pieces, unless they look miniature in the room, should be removed. Rarely do we find a room too big needing filling, but mostly finds rooms too full and in need of editing.

Traffic flow must have proper flow from the entrance of the room to the access of the next rooms. It also should include a way to get to the exterior views easily and not be hindered by furniture. When Staging we have to consider that the buyer is going to want to see the yard and surroundings to get a feel for what they are buying. It helps them to feel comfortable.

Traffic flow is created by removal of extra furniture and correct placement of the existing pieces, which of course is different in every room, in every house. Generally, there are always two to four traffic flows in each room: the primary flow through the room, then all of the secondary flows like access to closets, windows and desk/sitting areas.

JUSTIN'S COMMENTS:

In order to maximize the impact of your floor plan and make the best first impression, calling a professional Home Stager is a key step in ensuring your home is showcased in the most positive light. Floor plans can be complicated and the concepts of interior decorating come into play when addressing these issues, as visual balance and flow need to play off each other properly.

There's nothing worse for a seller than having a buyer walk into a room with too much furniture and feel crowded, or worse, feel "lost" in a room that has no distinct "purpose". I've seen many home owners try their best to achieve that "show home" quality to their home. In the end, it would've been a better decision (and a quicker one!) to call a Home Stager to get the job done right, the first time.

BEFORE

AFTER

ACTUAL WORK BY JILL'S TEAM:

"These are examples of an occupied home: master bedroom and kitchen.

We utilized the client's furniture and our accessories

They still lived in the home with their small child, did everything I asked them to do and they sold in 4 days."

BEFORE

AFTER

CHAPTER 8

Kitchen, Kitchen, Kitchen!

"The kitchen is the heart of the home - How do you make it stand out and shine? What elements does your team focus on?"

Jill says:

Kitchens always carry weight when selling a property as the buyer knows that they will be spending a lot of time there and also knows that the financial investment required to update them is quite large. It is one of the biggest ticket items on a property.

Television programs on Home Staging have conditioned buyers to want what they see on TV, and what this means for sellers is that they need to produce wow factor kitchens, or risk losing a sale.

Depending on your budget, you should invest a large portion to making the kitchen have great appeal. Beyond de-cluttering, you need to take a hard look at condition and age of fixtures. A kitchen should be 0-5 years old. And even that is pushing it.

Consider updating cabinets if you can, or at least appliances. If you can't afford new appliances then the should at least be shiny clean and in working order. There

41

is nothing worse then a buyer opening your fridge to see an over stuffed buffet of week old leftovers with a 'smell'. CLEAN, CLEAN, CLEAN those appliances as they are part of your selling package.

Countertops, back splashes, new hardware and lighting will also produce a nice result. The interiors of cabinetry should be clean, in good condition or freshly painted and all surfaces free of grease, food or knife damage.

When painting cabinets you MUST follow the correct process, or you will end up with a disaster on your final product. A professional painting company should know how to properly apply paint to cabinetry and what the correct prep process is. Go through multiple interviews on this subject, as it is not worth it to make mistakes.

Chips in counters or missing hinges, handles, greasy fans and yellowed linoleum all scream 'Money Needed Here!!" And a buyer will move onto greener pastures to find a new home that doesn't require much effort or expense upon arrival.

Buyers today know what they want and do not have the desire or extra cash to make changes, so unless you give them what they are looking for they will simply buy your competition or give you a very low offer so they can have money to bring it up to current standards. It really is your choice. Do you either reduce your price to reflect the thousands required for the updates? Or do you do the updates for less to obtain true market value? Buyers always think in thousands and the truth is a house is only worth what a BUYER is willing to pay for it, not what a seller wants for it.

The demand of buyers is telling us that newer kitchens are what they want.

The ROI for a kitchen update is 176% according to a Home Gain 2011 survey, so whatever you invest, you will make a return on.

A final thought, kitchen Staging should reflect a lifestyle selling element. So who are your buyers? How do you appeal to their needs? What would they be looking for in a new property? Staging with this mind will help you to add fixtures and final touches that will sell.

JUSTIN'S COMMENTS:

The trend I see when talking with my buyer clients is that more and more the kitchen is becoming the "hub" of the home. It's the space where meals are cooked, kids do homework, guests are entertained, and where meaningful conversations are held long into the night. It's also the one room that is connected to various other rooms in the home, whether it's the living room, family room, dining room, or front foyer.

Ensuring that your Home Stager has experience in making kitchens look their absolute best is imperative if you want your home to stand out from the competition. If your budget allows, updating your kitchen to reflect current trends is a good call, even if it means replacing appliances, counter tops, and painting cabinets. A bit more time spent beforehand can save weeks or even months of languishing on the market because your home *"is really nice....but that kitchen just won't do."*

BEFORE

AFTER

CHAPTER 9

Ugly Bathroom, Pretty Bathroom

*"Jill, bathrooms are such a personal thing - How do I
ensure I highlight my bathrooms best features??*

*What are some common ugly points that many sellers
fail to miss when cleaning/preparing a bathroom when
selling their home?"*

Jill says:

Bathrooms need to carry impact for a number of reasons. They are personal
space, can get very dirty and smelly and we really don't want to know what
you are doing in there...So remove all reading material!

They must be so clean it's like they are brand new. Every inch, including
behind the toilet, along baseboards and all edges of the shower and plumbing
fixtures need to be sparkling clean. This is also true for the fan, lighting
and cabinetry.

Take the time to empty out and really clean them, as well as apply a fresh
coat of mould resistant paint on the ceilings and walls. Old flaking paint
needs to be removed properly, re-sanded, primed and painted so it reflects a

professional paint job. Mould issues must be addressed, not covered over. Tile grouting should be really clean and repaired wherever required. Re-grouting can be done if the tile is not broken to give it a fresh look. If tiles are broken or there are older fixtures, they should be updated to reflect current trends.

Painting the cabinets or updating the whole thing will also impress buyers, just make sure not to paint hinges! As well, all plumbing should be in good working order.

Taking care of small and large details says that you cared about your property and will ensure a faster sale.

JUSTIN'S COMMENTS:

Although a buying decision is ultimately up to my clients, as a real estate agent I do take note of these little details when going through a property. If I see that they've spruced the property up with new trim and paint, but the nail holes aren't filled and there are gaps in between the joints, I know that they've likely rushed the job. This makes me question what else was overlooked during the time the sellers have owned the property.

In the same light, if a bathroom has a new vanity, mirror, and lighting, but if a light bulb is burnt out, there's no caulking at the edges of the counter top, and the mirror is hung crooked, it makes me question if the same lack of attention was paid to the plumbing. **Always keep in mind: *There are <u>DOLLARS</u> to be made in tending to the <u>DETAILS</u>*.**

BEFORE

ACTUAL WORK BY JILL'S TEAM:

"This client's home was listed over $900,000.00 and located in a sought after area.

All parts of the home were renovated expect this bathroom.

They took my advice on updates and did preparation for 3 weeks to get ready.

They had us come in for full property staging at the end and sold immediately."

AFTER

CHAPTER 10

On Closets
And Clutter

"When it comes to closets, what is the best way to ensure you impress buyers, the FIRST time they peek inside?"

Jill Says:

Great question: Think of it as unwrapping a new gift on Christmas morning...Will you be pleased with what you open? Will a look of surprise be on your face or shock? Or will it be a disappointment?

Linen, bedroom and front closets are areas buyers do look in, because they are buying them! And so preparation of those areas needs to be considered of course. Smells, like footwear, moth balls or hockey gear will turn any stomach. So de-clutter all extras, clean it really well and organize!

Use baskets to get a handle on smaller items, stack "like" things together, color-co ordinate and the results will be a pleasing "present"-ation to your buyer! Just like unwrapping a new gift!

JUSTIN'S COMMENTS:

Although closets seem like such a smaller aspect of getting your home ready for sale, I can attest to what Jill says here.

I can't recall how many times I've taken buyers through a fantastic home, only to have them label it as "*The Smelly Hockey House*" or the "*Grandma Moth Ball*" house. Having peculiar smells in any closet is at worst, a huge turn off and at best, just another item that will leave a negative impression on the buyers that come through your home.

And smells are just part of it. One of the trends I see continuing far into the future as more families are living together is the need for adequate storage. By organizing and arranging the items in your closets to maximize the impression of "spacious storage", you'll be ahead of your competitors on the market who may have a nice kitchen and living room, but have jammed their bedroom and hall closets with all their "junk" and negated any positive impression their home may have had on a buyer.

ACTUAL WORK BY JILL'S TEAM:

"Laundry Room Shelves....Shows how any closet shelf system can be organized to still be functional during selling and have a better visual impact."

BEFORE

AFTER

CHAPTER 11

Have A Home Office? This Chapter is For YOU

"I run a home-business out of my house, and my office is my workspace - What's the best way to ensure I can still get work done, but keep the room in top-shape for showings?"

Jill says:

Home offices are always a challenge. Working in a Staged space requires a few things. First, as always: De-clutter. This includes diplomas, mail and awards. Anything that links you to the home, even utility bills should be removed from sight.

Make sure all unnecessary computer equipment, boxes, binders and extra cords are all packed. Keep out only the essentials for while you are selling. Use drawers for your small office related items and keep only a computer, phone, and lamp on the desk. A filing cabinet, fax and copier are fine to have out as you still need them but just keep it to a minimum. Also avoid bulletin boards, calendars, family pictures, and of course client information or clues to the type of work you do. Keep in mind that you do not want your personal or business information to influence your negotiations with a snoopy buyer.

Home offices are part of our norm in our society so they should look comfortable and inviting with well placed accessories and greenery, art and beautifully Staged bookshelves that add to the "WOW" factor.

JUSTIN'S COMMENTS:

Speaking as one that has his own home office, I can empathize with sellers who are now saddled with the task of de-cluttering and arranging the "chaotic organization" that we all seem to operate amidst in our home offices. (*Okay, maybe it's just me that's cluttered and you're a tidy-Tom!*)

However you operate in your workspace, I'm reminded of a comment that keeps coming up in conversations with Jill as we wrote this book, and that is:

*"How we live in a home, and how we get that home **SOLD** for top dollar, are two **VERY** different things."*

While you may be running a business from your home, keep in mind the reasons and end-benefit of why you're making a transition, and this will be motivation to keep your "*War Room*" in tip-top shape. After all, it's only for a little while until your home sells!

BEFORE

ACTUAL WORK BY JILL'S TEAM:

"This occupied home office needed Staging using the home owners' furniture and our props.

We had a budget to work with and accomplished our goal, addressing traffic flow to the closet which was blocked by a cabinet.

We removed the dated valances and created a space that helped sell this house!"

AFTER

ACTUAL PHOTOS OF JILL'S WORK: "Vacant home office photo."

CHAPTER 12

The Garage, AKA "Man Cave"

"Home Staging is about the home, but what about the Garage? My husband thinks that 'nobody cares about the garage....and it's the man-space, so having it clean isn't important...'

Is he right? Do garages matter? Should we be doing anything to enhance the appeal of our garage?"

Jill says:

Garages are important and make just as much of an impact as any other part of the home as they show off what kind of storage there is for children's bikes, shovels, cars, and Christmas ornaments. If your garage is packed full and barely fits your cars, then your are saying to buyers that "it's too small."

A full de-clutter of this space will allow buyers to see the space better. Things like bikes, hockey gear and nets, toys, tools and recycling should all be removed. Also remove sports memorabilia and any possibly offensive posters. Use the existing shelving you have for any items that need to remain on site while selling, otherwise - pack it and move to storage.

One of the biggest issues with garages these days is that they really are not built big enough for one car to comfortably fit, let alone two. So maximize the space you do have.

As well clean up oil spills from your car, using Coca Cola®. Sweep, pressure wash, and clean flooring. Also, no more smoking in the garage! Fix broken windows, freshen up door paint, make sure all lighting is bright and working and create a garage space that any man would love so you will stand out from your competitors!

JUSTIN'S COMMENTS:

In a climate such as ours, where it routinely his -25 or -30 Celcius in the winter time, having a garage to keep the snow off your vehicle(s) for the 4-6 months (*or even 8 months some years!*) is a HUGE selling point that buyers consider.

Being able to fit two full-size vehicles, or a full-size car and full-size truck, in the confines of a standard double garage is a big deciding factor for many buyers with families, or for those who just need that extra storage (*and who doesn't??*).

I'd echo Jill's sentiments: I find that my buyers look favorably on a home when the garage is tidy, de-cluttered, the lights work, the vehicles can fit, and there's no cigarette or pet smells!

CHAPTER 13

Home Staging For Estate Sales

"I'm handling the sale of an estate. What are the best ways you can position hiring a Home Stager to the executor of someone who has just passed? How can I overcome the potential insult/disrespect of wanting to 'move and re-arrange' the deceased's belongings?"

Jill says:

Typically in these sensitive situations there has been enough time passed that the family knows they need to look at taking the next steps. Usually, unless there are major internal issues, most families are making joint decisions on what to do and lots of time and discussion will have to take place.

As a Stager, I have encountered this and request all decision makers are present if possible for my consultation, even if they are on the phone with us from a distance and have reviewed my website.

My information is presented equally to all parties and I can answer everyone's questions.

The process for consulting and Staging is still the same, but may take a little longer as the idea sinks in. After all there are many people hurting and they all may have strong feelings or memories attached to this home, positive or negative, and this will affect how they proceed.

Upgrades and rentals are likely to be required due to the age of the property or the old style of furniture, although that is not always they case.

Usually getting the home to a clean slate works best, that way the family also sees it with new furniture and props and it helps them to emotionally let go.

Most often, unless upgrades were done in the last five years, changes will need to be considered. The benefit to family working together is that they can pool their resources and usually, if they are united, they can accomplish a lot in a short time.

The younger generations understand the benefits to Staging and so I treat them as a regular client that needs to make choices within their budget.

They will need to divide furniture and property among themselves and I am not involved in that. If we are using the existing furniture, we are usually all on the same page by then.

If there are any disputes about packing, donations, and removal or moving items it is usually the result of one person, still hurting, or have personal agendas against the progress. In that case, I cannot force, only make all my suggestions, answer questions, be compassionate and not pressure their choices. I respect their needs but do not get involved in settling internal disputes.

Estates can be a longer more difficult process depending on the hundreds of other factors in the background, but I still approach it with one goal....how can we get this ready, Staged and sold in the shortest time frame for the best price?

JUSTIN'S COMMENTS:

Dealing with the passing of a loved one can be a hard time. Add to this the added burden of selling their property and you have a recipe for undue stress.

With that being said, I've never met anyone who, prior to passing on, had any intention of making life difficult for those they're leaving behind.

As a real estate agent, my job is to educate my clients and empower them to make the best decisions for their situation. One of the ways I accomplish this is to take away as much stress from the process as possible. Having a professional Home Stager take care of the details of preparing an estate home for sale is, in my opinion as a real estate agent, a wise choice that takes much of the stress of selling out of the equation.

Not only do you increase the chances of realizing a higher price for the home and maximizing the proceeds for any heirs/charities/trusts that are beneficiaries, you are also more likely to attract higher quality buyers and get the job done faster when Professional Home Staging is coupled with aggressive marketing and up-to-the-minute market research by your real estate agent.

BEFORE

ACTUAL WORK BY JILL'S TEAM:

Though this was not an estate property, it is a good example of a "...Dated master bedroom painted with sponge painting (very out of style!)

We had (the seller) paint in a new neutral and we brought all the accessories & furniture for the Staged look.

Master bedrooms should really have (a contemporary) "wow" factor as they are a key room for a buyer."

AFTER

CHAPTER 14

GOT CONDO?

"I can see how Home Staging would make a HOUSE look really good, but I've got just a small condo - Does Staging a condo make a big difference?"

Jill says:

Home Staging affects each property positively. This is because de-cluttering, repairs, paint, lighting and updates are all taken care of for starters.

Secondly, and most importantly, the interior photos on the internet are more interesting and have more "wow" factor than those that are not staged. 98% of today's buyers search the net first BEFORE calling an real estate agent. This means that they are <u>weeding out</u> the ones they don't want to see!

So all things being equal from a price, location and size standpoint- that then leaves presentation as the next deciding factor in which one they will ask to see. So the question remains, is your competition Staged? And if they are, you should be. If they are not, you should be because then you stand out.

Smaller condos, larger homes, and everything in between all benefit from Professional Staging services.

Some smaller condos also are not properly fitted with furniture and then it looks even smaller and it turns off a buyer. Our goal is to create the best layout using our furniture plan, and accessories. This shows buyers how they can live comfortably in a small space. It creates an atmosphere that a buyer falls in love with and it encourages an offer, faster.

JUSTIN'S COMMENTS:

While Staging your detached home is an integral part of achieving maximum value in any market, I'd go so far as to say it's a necessity when preparing your condo unit to be placed on the market for sale.

Here's why:

While many subdivisions have similar houses and layouts all built by the same handful of builders, think about how condos are built:

One developer. Same layouts on nearly every floor. One above the other, with the only exceptions being the top floor units. At least in a subdivision, you have to go up and down the street to find houses that are similar or identical to yours. In a condo, you need only look at the floors above or below you...*All at the same address!*

Unless you're a penthouse or sub-penthouse, chances are very likely that there are many units in your building (even if you're in a low-rise or mid-rise building vs. high-rise) that are identical to yours in terms of square footage, layout, and original finishings.

Home Staging allows you to differentiate yourself from the masses, not just in your building or development, but the abundance of other units that are competing for the same pool of buyers.

ACTUAL WORK BY JILL'S TEAM:

"This vacant condo was Staged with rented items.

Color co-ordinated relating to the fixed elements of the property shows off this condo with impact and wow factor."

The elements Jill is showcasing in this photo are absolutely stunning and make the difference between having a drab condo that gets no showings, and having a condo where buyers rush to view and make an offer.

While we were writing this book, Jill did a similar job for a client of mine who had an executive condo in a downtown hi-rise. End Result: The unit sold in half the average time, during a down market, with two offers from very excited buyers. If you have a condo - Get it Staged!

The color version of the above photo is available along with many others at:

www.StrategicTipsForHomeSellers.com

CHAPTER 15

How To Choose The BEST Home Stager For The Job

"There's so many people getting into the industry, how do I choose the best Home Stager for me? What are the typical fees? Is there a benefit to hiring a more expensive Home Stager??

Jill says:

The Home Staging industry is not a regulated one, so finding a good home stager is really up to you to do your research. When interviewing a Stager first note if they are charging for their consultations or not. If they are, they are more likely operating a reputable business. Stagers that are 'free consulters' really are not going to provide you what you need. You do get what you pay for in this sense.

During a consultation valuable information on how to prepare for Home Staging, discussions on renovations, color and repairs are going to be discussed and should be paid for, as it is part of the professional services a Home Stager should offer. Your Staging consultant needs to have experience with these processes.

A 'Free Consultation' is really a good indicator that someone is new to Staging and most likely won't be able to give you advice based on expertise and experience.

Home Stagers should also have business alliances with flooring and painting companies, as well as carpet and interior cleaners.

Home Stagers should also have a portfolio online or in their computer that they can show you their actual projects. A 'true portfolio' and not 'stock photography' is what you need to look for. If you hire a Stager based on stock photos, beware, they are not showcasing their own work and if you expect those results you will not get it.

Another key point to ask about is client testimonials, referrals from past clients and referrals from your real estate agent. This goes a long way to indicate if they have a solid foundation of experience to truly help you. Remember, you're dealing with the equity in your property and it is important not to entrust it to just a 'fly by night' Home Stager.

The industry is full of talented Stagers who have never taken a professional staging course, and do have the ability to put your house together well, however there are many that are not as talented.

If your stager has taken any courses towards learning more about how to Stage properly, and how to operate a Professional Staging business, that will be a benefit to you.

One Staging course is not better than another, as it still depends on the individual taking that course and if they are naturally talented and professional. This is why a detailed discussion on their experience, review of their portfolio and speaking to past clients will really help. If they are professional, they will not be intimidated by your questions, and will be able to give you answers.

When it comes to pricing for Staging there are so many factors. Cheaper is not better, let's start there.

Staging fees usually range from $1,500.00 to $5,000.00 depending on the size of your home, plus monthly furniture and accessory rentals, deliveries and of course any other work done such as painting, flooring upgrades etc.

If you are getting pricing for Staging fees less than that chances are they are not offering the Staging talent that will help you sell.

If you want your Staging project successfully executed it pays to pay for it! Otherwise you will be paying a low Staging fee for something you really could have done yourself.

JUSTIN'S COMMENTS:

In my years of dealing with buyers and sellers, I find that the most successful individuals are those who understand two kinds of PAIN:

The Pain of <u>Achievement</u>

And

The Pain of <u>Regret</u>

Those who understand "The Pain of Achievement" know that in life, good things aren't free. You have to invest something valuable (time, finances, emotion) in order to see any value come out the other end. This is what motivates an Olympic athlete to train at 3am. It's what motivates an honor's student to study hard when their friends are out at the movies. It's what enables a good parent to understand that, while their kid is saying a lot of hurtful things right now, that sticking to their guns now will ensure they raise a responsible adult later.

These successful people also understand "The Pain of Regret", which means they'd rather invest what they need to now to reap a reward in the future, because the consequences of not investing that value ahead of time means they'll experience far greater pain in the future when they don't achieve what they wanted.

Educated buyers understand that they need to pay good value (fair market price) for a home that is good value (one they'll enjoy living in, that fits their budget and their lifestyle).

Educated sellers also understand that in order to achieve that top-market value for their home, that investing in the front-end with the services of a talented Home Stager will reap many tangible and intangible benefits in the end.

Compare our marketplace to other mega-metro areas like Los Angeles, New York, or Vancouver. In a city where homes routinely sell for $1 million, $5 million, $10 million and more, it's not uncommon for sellers to pay a professional Home Stager in the neighbourhood of TENS of THOUSANDS of dollars. In fact, I recently watched an episode on a popular reality series where a seller spent close to $50,000 on a Home Stager to get her ocean front property sold...And it wasn't a mega-8-figure-home either!

The most successful sellers I've dealt with are those who are educated on the market and that understand that one way or another, you've got to pay. You pay the "Pain of Achievement" or you pay for convenience now and reap the "Pain of Regret" later. *Either way, you always get what you pay for.*

If you want cheap transportation, ride a bike or take the bus...

If you want to save money on groceries, there's always macaroni...

But to get the best positioning and presentation for your home, especially in a challenging market, it doesn't hurt to consider spending good money on the great service from a Professional Home Stager.

CHAPTER 16

Friend Or Foe? Why You Should Hire A PRO

"My friend watches a lot of HGTV ™ or TLC ™ and has a really good knack for design, why should I use a professional Home Stager instead of having my friend come by? Does the industry have any standards/ associations I should be aware of?"

Jill says:

The Home Staging industry is an un-regulated industry, which means that anyone can start a Staging business and be a "Home Stager". This is where reviews of portfolios and speaking to a Stager's past clients will ensure you're dealing with a true professional who can get the job done properly.

Hiring a professional Home Stager over having a friend do it for it will benefit you greatly. A Stager is in the MARKETING business, not the decorating business, and many factors play into this being a better choice than having a friend come by playing 'designer'.

Key points that a Stager considers are:

 Who is the target market they're trying to appeal to?

What the price point is and the look that is expected by a buyer?
What colors and furniture co-ordination do various rooms require?

Beyond that Stagers have resources for rentals that the public does not have. This will enable you to rent items, instead of buying and ultimately save you money.

A Stager takes this process serious and should deliver results that will bring you offers. A friend, perhaps well meaning and possibly capable, does not fully understand the sales and marketing aspect or trends and could in fact, make it look worse. This could affect friendships especially if you need to hire a professional after a few weeks of not selling.

My recommendations would be to keep the personal friendships out of the business choice to maximize equity. It will save you a potentially uncomfortable situation later.

JUSTIN'S COMMENTS:

As a real estate agent, my industry is a licensed profession, meaning not anyone can just claim to be "in business". Even still, with all the rules and regulations governing the real estate industry, it's imperative that buyers and sellers interview an agent to ensure the right "fit" by reviewing what track record they have, checking out testimonials, marketing plans, etc.

In the same way, when a seller is selecting a professional Home Stager, they need to ensure that they check the Stager's testimonials, portfolio of past work, and any certifications or designations they have. Another great question to ask a Stager you're considering hiring is:

"Have you been in business for a while, or did you just jump into the industry when the market got hot and it was easy to get a home sold?"

A true Professional Home Stager will be able to demonstrate that they've can provide immense value to their clients both during and prior to any market upswing, as well as in the wake of a market downturn.

BEFORE

ACTUAL WORK BY JILL'S TEAM:

"This home was listed just under $1-million in a down market. Notice the gym in the master suite and the disproportionate furniture and accessories.

We corrected the scale of the room by adding appropriately sized accessories and removed the gym equipment.

The home sold in under three weeks."

AFTER

ACTUAL WORK BY JILL'S TEAM:

"Child's bedroom in the same home (*refer to Pg. 87*).

We had them de-clutter, paint into a neutral and of course stage.

Results were a sold house in the first couple of weeks!"

BEFORE

AFTER

GLOSSARY OF TERMS

CURB APPEAL

"The first impression of the front yard when arriving at the house."

DE-CLUTTER

"To remove all unnecessary items off the property while selling, creating more space and giving the buyer a better look at what you are selling."

GROUT

"Gritty substance used in tile floor applications. Comes in a variety of colors."

HOME STAGER

"A qualified professional that can accurately assess the needs of a property and execute them with speed, talent, and marketing ability."

HOME STAGING

"Presenting a listed property in the best condition, to secure the highest possible selling price."

ROI

"Return-On-Investment"

SCALE

"The way objets relate to each other in a room. Color and size/shape affect the scale."

SIGHT LINES

"What your eye can see from a stationary point of view."

STOCK PHOTOGRAPHY

"Photos bought or taken from other's website for image creating purposes and not usually reflective of projects completed by the Home Stager.

TRAFFIC PATTERNS

"Access by foot through a room from Point A to Point B. When selling a house, traffic patterns need to flow to closets, windows, and other rooms."

TRUE PORTFOLIO

"Actual photography of projects that were complete by the Home Stager."

VISUAL WEIGHT

"The ability of an element to draw attention to itself. Often this is created through the use of color and/or contrast."

"WOW" FACTOR

"What comes out of a buyer's mouth when they are truly impressed!"

AUTHOR BIO'S

About Jill Gargus - "Simply Irresistible Interiors Inc."

Founded in 2003, "Simply Irresistible Interiors Inc." is the largest Home Staging company in the Edmonton area, offering Home Staging Training, Furniture and Accessory Rentals and Full Service Staging.

As a former real-estate-agent-turned-Home Stager, Jill Gargus knows what it takes to get your home sold. With an abundance of talent in the Staging arena she also teaches other's what she knows. Jill holds Staging Certificates from multiple organizations and is a certified "Dewey Color Consultant™".

Jill and her Home Staging team have Staged hundreds of homes since 2003. Their specialty is in creating an atmosphere that a buyer will fall in love with, resulting in top-dollar-offers, regardless of the adverse market conditions sellers may be facing.

Information on Simply Irresistible Interiors Inc. and services they offer may be found in the resource section at the back of this book.

About Justin LaFavor - Author, Real Estate Agent

Justin has been serving his client-base of first time buyers, repeat sellers, as well as new and seasoned investors, since early 2006.

In the years since, Justin has received numerous awards for his accomplishments, become a top-producer at his brokerage, and gone on to sell everything from a $3,000 mobile home, to a million-dollar estate home, and everything in between.

With a passion for marketing, and a dedication to client education, Justin has a professional mission to:

> *"Empower clients to reach their goals by educating them about their choices and engaging them with five-star excellence in customer service."*

Justin has created *"The Better Buyer"* & *"The Savvy Seller"* seminar programs, and authored two books by the same titles (slated for release in early-mid 2012) to help prepare buyers and sellers to make the best decisions possible to reach their goals. Information on these, as well as other books Justin has written, can be found in the resources section at the back of this book.

RESOURCES
& CONTACT
INFORMATION

RESOURCES &
CONTACT INFORMATION

HOME STAGING 101

Home Staging 101 is a one day class designed for home owners who are ambitious enough to tackle their entire home staging project from start to finish, including the actual staging placement of furniture and props. It is fun, very informative and will teach a seller how to layout their rooms, choose paint colors, de-clutter and also accessorize correctly. Not for the weak in heart!

Visit **www.StageAndSell.ca** for details or call Jill at **780.452.4527**

THE BETTER BUYER SEMINAR

The Better Buyer seminar was developed in response to the growing need for education for buyers in the Edmonton real estate market. Throughout the seminar, attendees will learn how to avoid the pitfalls and "rookie" mistakes many buyers make when purchasing a home...Mistakes that could potentially cost thousands of dollars!

In addition to a Q&A session with Justin, attendees will have "live" access to industry professionals who can answer their questions in an open and honest manner.

Best of all, no selling is done at the seminar. It's the perfect way for buyers to prepare themselves to get the best deal on the right house, and save themselves as much stress, hassle, (and money!) as possible.

Visit **www.TheBetterBuyer.ca** for details or call **1.800.216.8228 ext.1180**

THE SAVVY SELLER SEMINAR

The Savvy Seller seminar aims to equip both first time and repeat home sellers with the tools, market analysis, and perspectives that will enable them to:

-Get their property sold for top dollar
-Achieve success in a time frame that suits their goals
-Minimize the "headaches" associated with your average real estate transaction.

Graduates will walk away with an understanding of the three key points on the "Successful Home-Sale Pyramid", and will also receive copies of Justin's book in addition to a home-study workbook to help them navigate the steps any seller needs to take prior to putting their home on the market.

Visit **www.TheSavvySeller.ca** for details of call **1.800.216.8228 ext. 1280**

SEARCHING FOR YOUR NEXT HOME?

Search All Edmonton & Area Listings INSTANTLY Like Justin Does As A Real Estate Agent - 24/7 - No Hassle - No Obligation - "No-Pushy-Sales-Tactics" GUARANTEED! *Sign Up Today At*:

www.EdmontonListingsBrowser.com

CONTACT INFO

Jill Gargus can be reached via the following:

PHONE: 780.452.4527

EMAIL: homestaging@telus.net

WEB: www.StageAndSell.ca & www.TheStagingShop.com

Justin LaFavor can be reached via the following:

PHONE: 1.800.216.8228 ext. 0180 (Private Voice Mailbox)

EMAIL: justin@edmonton-real-estate-online.com

WEB: www.GotEdmontonRealEstate.com

NOTES:

Made in the USA
Charleston, SC
28 November 2011